Crayola

Our COLORFUL World

A CRAYOLA CELEBRATION OF COLOR

Mari Schuh

Lerner Publications ◆ Minneapolis

CONTENTS

A World of Color

Look around. What colors do you see? There's **red** and **yellow**, **blue** and **green**, and all the colors in between.

The world is bursting with color. Let's take a look!

Hello, Red!

Look closely.
Where can you find **red**?

Scarlet, **brick red**, and **maroon** are all shades of **red**. **Red** is all around you!

Red **Animals**

Red perches high in the trees. Cardinals and strawberry finches find juicy berries on a cold winter day.

Red moves in many ways.
Crabs walk sideways on the wet,
rocky shore.

Watch them go!

Red can be tiny.
A small ladybug crawls across
a plant. Do you see it?

Red **Foods**

Red is ripe and ready to eat! Pick juicy tomatoes off the vine. Find apples in the orchard.

Share strawberries
with a friend.
Red is so good to eat.

Red can be a sweet celebration. Creamy frosting and fluffy cakes are yummy desserts.

Enjoy every bite!

Red **Where You Live**

Red helps keep us safe. Stop signs tell drivers it's time to stop. Bright **red** signs are easy to see.

Red comes to the rescue! Fire trucks rush down the street. They put out fires fast.

Cruise around in a **red** sports car. **Red** can be fast and fun!

You can see **red** on holidays. **Red** plants are popular at Christmas. People decorate with **red** for good luck during Chinese New Year.

Red is on the move!
Ride in a red wagon.
Spot red bikes around town.

Where will you see red today?

Color with Red!

Grab some **red** crayons.

Draw a picture using only the color **red**.

How many different shades will you use?

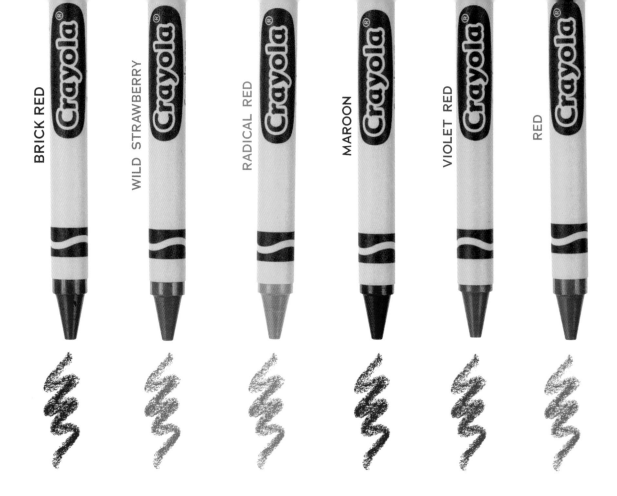

BRICK RED

WILD STRAWBERRY

RADICAL RED

MAROON

VIOLET RED

RED

Red All around You

Red is found almost everywhere. Here are some Crayola®
crayon shades of **red** used in this book. Can you find them
in the photos? Which shade of **red** do you like the best?

Hello, Yellow!

Do you see **yellow** around you?

Our world is full of beautiful **yellow**. **Gold**, **canary**, and **lemon** are all shades of **yellow**.

Yellow **in Nature**

Yellow lights up the sky! The golden sun shines brightly on a warm summer day. Leaves glow in the trees.

Some leaves turn yellow in the fall.
Slowly, they fall to the ground.

See them pile up!

Sunflowers grow tall in a country field. Their flowers move toward the sun.

Yellow **Animals**

Yellow crawls across the ground. The bright skin of lizards and salamanders stands out against the grass.

See **yellow** buzzing around colorful flowers. Bumblebees sip sweet nectar.

Cheep! Cheep!

Yellow can be soft and fluffy. Cute chicks have fuzzy feathers called down.

Yellow **Foods**

People enjoy **yellow** foods at picnics. Squirt **yellow** mustard on a corn dog. Snack on sweet peppers!

Spread butter on corn on the cob.
Yellow is so yummy!

Yellow **Where You Live**

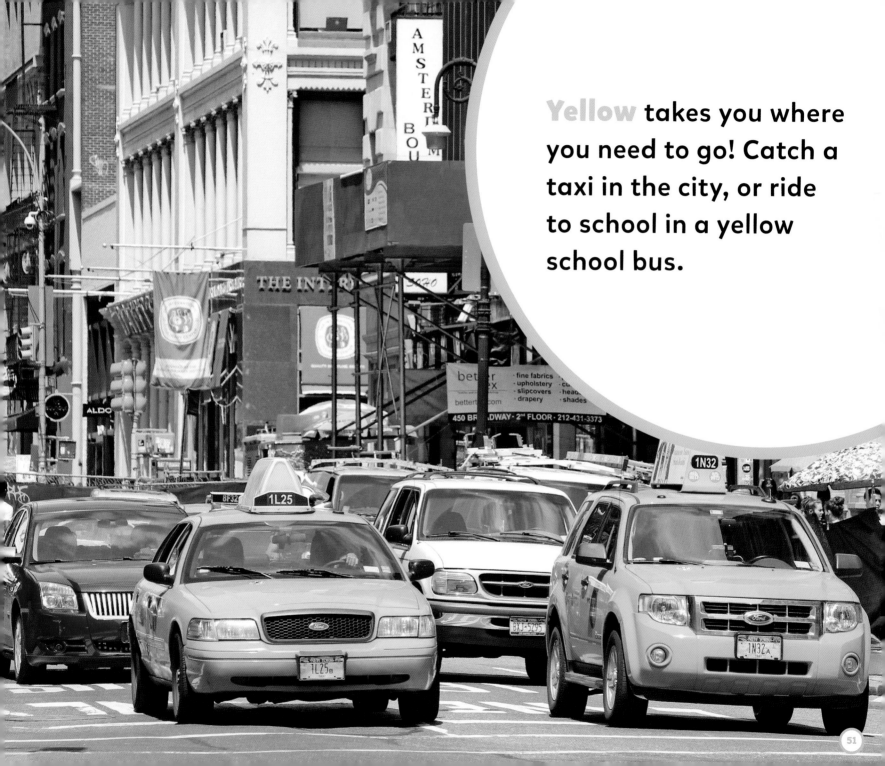

Yellow takes you where you need to go! Catch a taxi in the city, or ride to school in a yellow school bus.

Yellow signs help people on the road. They show us where to turn and where to cross. The bright color warns drivers to be careful.

Yellow is fun! Ride down a yellow slide. Wear a yellow uniform to play your favorite sport.

Where else can you see yellow?

Color with Yellow!

Draw a picture using only **yellow** crayons. What will you draw? How many shades will you use?

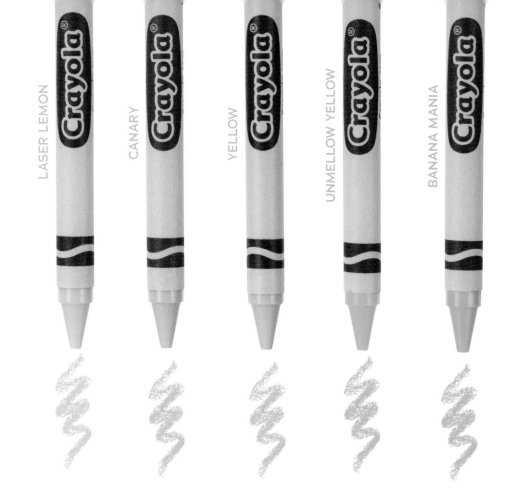

LASER LEMON

CANARY

YELLOW

UNMELLOW YELLOW

BANANA MANIA

Yellow All around You

Yellow is almost everywhere! Here are some Crayola®
crayon shades of yellow used in this book. Can you
find them in the photos?

Hello, Green!

Shades of **green** are all around.

Find **teal**, **olive**, **emerald**, **lime**, and **forest green**. **Green** is almost everywhere! Where do you see **green**?

Green in Nature

Green covers the forest trees. Fresh leaves open up for the sun.

Green grows in the hot, dry desert. Sharp spines cover prickly cactuses.

Be careful!

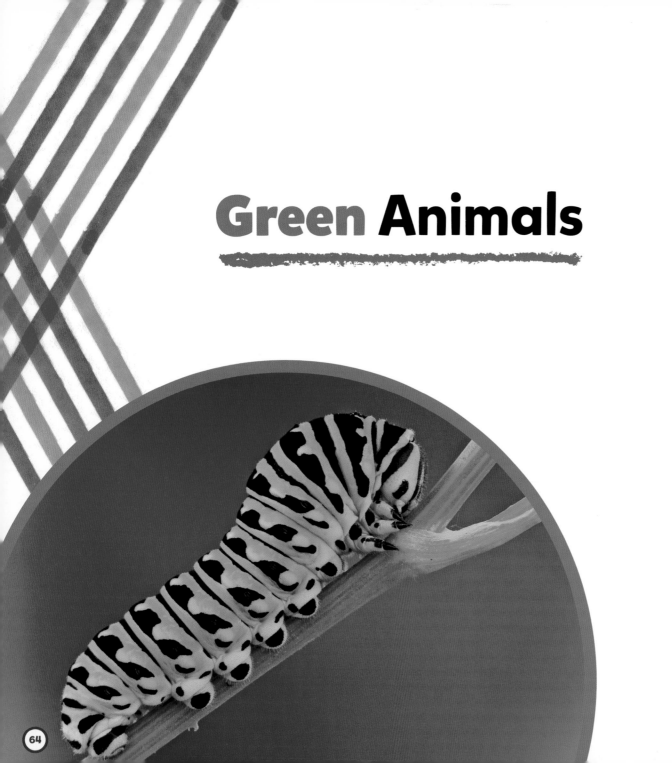

Green **Animals**

See **green** slither along the ground. Tiny scales protect snakes. Caterpillars munch on leaves.

Green peeks out from the pond.
Water keeps this frog's skin moist.

Ribbit! Ribbit!

Green parrots perch high in the trees. Lots of feathers keep them warm and dry.

Green **Foods**

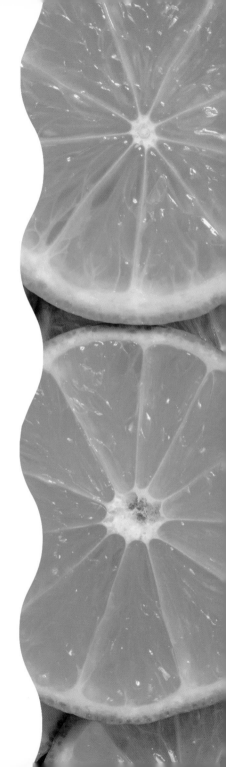

Green can be juicy. Apples, kiwis, and limes are tasty and good for you. Take a bite!

Green grows in the sun. Fill your plate with leafy lettuce. Nibble on plump **green** grapes.

Yum!

Ice cream, mints, and candies.
Green can be a special treat!
Which one is your favorite?

Green **Where You Live**

Green means go! It helps people on the move. Where will you go next?

You can find **green** where you play. Slide, bike, and climb. Have all sorts of fun with **green**!

Green is busy! Big machines work in the fields. Cars and buses zoom around town.

Where else can you find **green**?

Color with Green!

Draw a picture using only **green** crayons. What will you draw? What shades of **green** will you use?

ASPARAGUS

FERN

SHAMROCK

SEA GREEN

GREEN YELLOW

GRANNY SMITH APPLE

SCREAMIN' GREEN

Green All around You

Green is everywhere. Here are some Crayola® crayon shades of green used in this book. Can you find all of them in the photos? What's your favorite shade of green?

Hello, Blue!

Look around. Do you see **blue**?

Navy, **royal blue**, **denim**, and **sky blue** are all shades of **blue**. The world is full of **blue**!

Blue in Nature

You can find **blue** growing in fields and gardens. Bright **blue** petals spread out in the warm summer sun.

Blue is for summer fun.

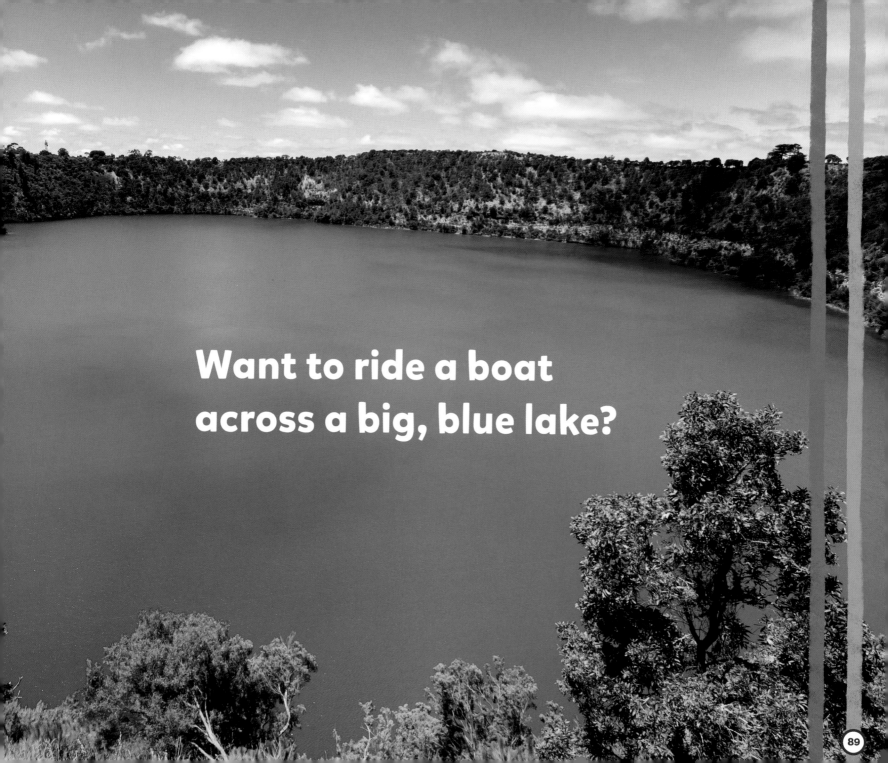

Want to ride a boat across a big, blue lake?

Look up!

Airplanes fly through **blue** way up high. See them zip across the sky.

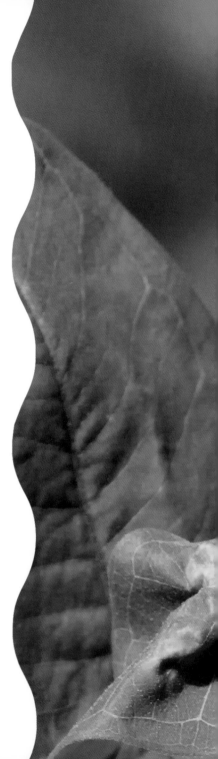

Blue Animals

Blue chirps in the trees. Bright feathers keep blue jays and buntings warm and dry.

Blue can be a warning. The rings of this **blue**-ringed octopus warn other animals to stay away!

Colorful **blue** betta fish swim through the dark water.

Blue **Foods**

Blue is fun to eat.
Plump blueberries
are a tasty treat.
Grab a handful!

Corn on the cob can be a beautiful **blue**.

Yum!

Blue
Where You Live

Blue is at school. It might be on your backpack or in your library. Where can you find **blue** in your classroom?

Blue runs up and down the field.
Uniforms bring a team together.
Helmets keep players safe.

Go, blue, go!

You can find **blue** close to home. Go for a ride on a **blue** bicycle at the park. Send a birthday card in a blue mailbox.

Where will you find **blue** today?

Color with **Blue!**

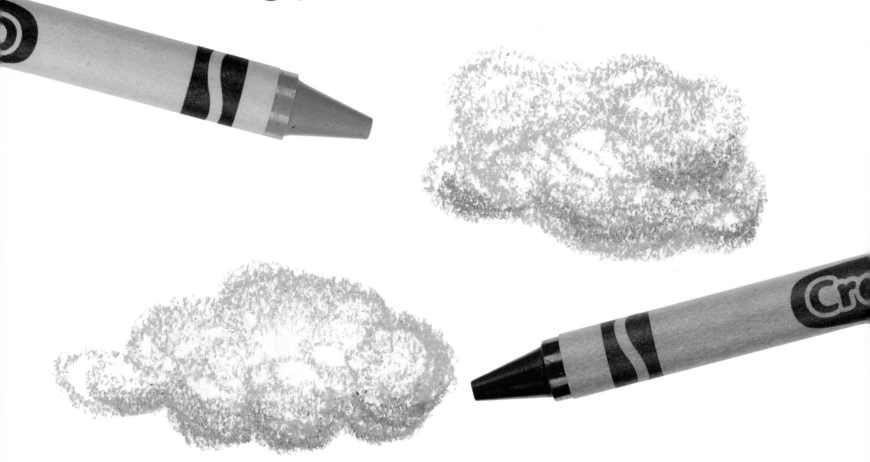

Draw a picture using only **blue** crayons.
What will you draw? How many shades of **blue** will you use?

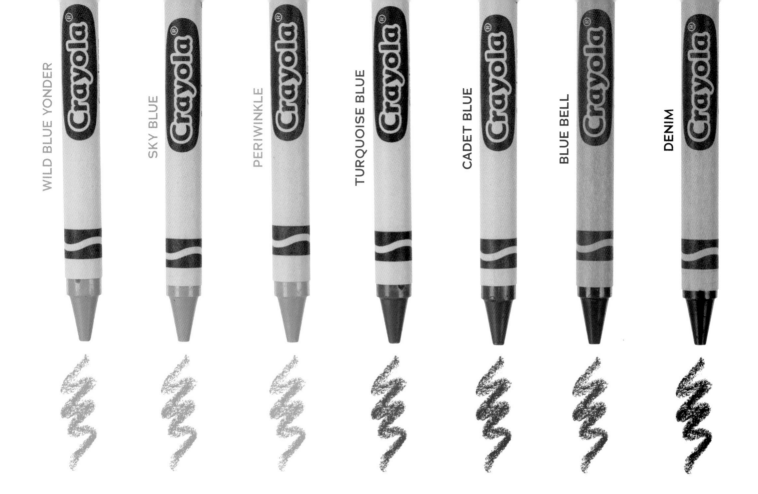

WILD BLUE YONDER

SKY BLUE

PERIWINKLE

TURQUOISE BLUE

CADET BLUE

BLUE BELL

DENIM

Blue All around Us

Blue is found all around our world. Here are some Crayola® crayon shades of **blue** used in this book. Can you find them in the photos? Which **blue** is your favorite?

Glossary

celebration: to observe in some special way

cob: the center part of an ear of corn on which the kernels grow

denim: a strong material used to make jeans and other pieces of clothing

down: a bird's soft, fluffy feathers

nectar: a sweet liquid that is found in many flowers

orchard: a field or farm where fruit trees are grown

perch: to stand on the edge of a branch or other object

poisonous: having a poison that can harm or kill

rescue: to save people and animals who are in danger

scale: a small, hard plate that covers a snake's body

shade: a color's lightness or darkness

spine: a sharp, pointy part of a plant or animal

uniform: special clothing worn by sports teams and other groups

warning: telling about a possible danger that might happen

Color with Crayola

For more fun, grab your markers and go to this website to find free coloring pages from Crayola:
https://www.crayola.com/featured/free-coloring-pages

Photo Credits

Image credits: GCapture/Shutterstock, p. 2 (strawberries); Kirill Zatrutin/Shutterstock, pp. 2, 44 (chicks); Tyler Fox/Shutterstock, pp. 3, 64 (caterpillar); fullemptyShutterstock, pp. 3, 84 (flower); Dirk Ercken/Shutterstock, pp. 5, 6 (frog); salajean/Shutterstock, pp. 5, 39 (sunflowers); Elovich/Shutterstock, p. 5 (blueberries); cuatrok77/Flickr (CC BY-SA 2.0), pp. 5, 69 (parrot); Davies and Starr/Photographer's Choice/Getty Images, p. 6 (lobster); smereka/Shutterstock, p. 7 (tractor); Kenneth Keifer/Shutterstock, p. 7 (leaf); Steven R Smith/Shutterstock, p. 8; Super Prin/Shutterstock, p. 9; vanchai/Shutterstock, p. 10; mikroman6/Moment/Getty Images, p. 13; Ed_H/Shutterstock, p. 14; V J Matthew/Shutterstock, p. 15; Lola Audu /Flickr (CC BY 2.0), p. 16; Lesya Dolyuk/Shutterstock, p. 19; Gregory Pelt/Shutterstock, p. 20; ND700/Shutterstock, p. 21; Tom Brandt/Flickr (CC BY 2.0), p. 22; Art Konovalov/Shutterstock, p. 25; BookyBuggy/Shutterstock, p. 26; Tatjana Alvegard/Stockbyte/Getty Images, p. 29; LisaValder/E+/Getty Images, p. 30 (heart, left); Nadezda Nikitina/Shutterstock, p. 32 (fish); SERGIY KUBYK/Shutterstock, p. 32 (duck); bergamont/Shutterstock, p. 32 (bananas); Tsekhmister/Shutterstock, p. 33 (chicks); mihalec/Shutterstock, p. 33 (combine); Ranglen/Shutterstock, p. 34; Chas Breton/Barcroft Media/Getty Images, p. 35; Robert CHG/Shutterstock, p. 36; Milos Batinic/Shutterstock, p. 37; Christian Schoissingeyer/Shutterstock, p. 40; Rainer Kaufung/McPhoto/ullstein bild/Getty Images, p. 41; HelloRF Zcool/Shutterstock, p. 43; Kwangmoozaa/Shutterstock, p. 46; GreenArt/Shutterstock, p. 47; GMVozd/E+/Getty Images, p. 48; Kovaleva_Ka/Shutterstock, p. 49; Mike Focus/Shutterstock, p. 50; Tupungato/Shutterstock, p. 51; Ken Hurst/Shutterstock, p. 52; BT.Suksan/Shutterstock, p. 53; romrodinka/iStock/Getty Images, p. 54; PNC/DigitalVision/Getty Images, p. 55; Studio Barcelona/Shutterstock, p. 56 (left); Yellow Stocking/Shutterstock, p. 56 (right); Smileus/Shutterstock, p. 58 (grass); languste/Shutterstock, p. 58 (chameleon); graja/Shutterstock, p. 59 (ice-cream bar); Elena Larina/Shutterstock, p. 59 (peas); VikaLugano/Shutterstock, p. 59 (flowers); ArTDi101/Shutterstock, p. 60; vovan/Shutterstock, p. 61; janniwet/Shutterstock, p. 62; arwenhuang/Shutterstock, p. 65; Michael Steden/Shutterstock, p. 66; Elena11/Shutterstock, p. 70; yuratosno3/Shutterstock, p. 71 (limes); grey_and/Shutterstock, p. 71 (apples); goodgold99/Shutterstock, p. 72; Tim UR/Shutterstock, p. 73; Africa Studio/Shutterstock, p. 74; JR T/Shutterstock, p. 75 (peppermint candy); Douglas Johns/StockFood Creative/Getty Images, p. 75 (ice-cream cone); IZZ HAZEL/Shutterstock, p. 76 (traffic light); Ken Wolter/Shutterstock, p. 77; Sergiy1975/Shutterstock, p. 79; smereka/Shutterstock, p. 80; Michael Shake/Shutterstock, p. 81; Ruslan Semichev/Shutterstock, p. 84 (jeans); Pan Xunbin/Shutterstock, p. 84 (lizard); Brocreative/Shutterstock, p. 85 (kids); Beth Swanson/Shutterstock, p. 85 (wave); PremiumArt/Shutterstock, p. 86; Shulevskyy Volodymyr/Shutterstock, p. 87; ian woolcock/Shutterstock, p. 89; GeoStock/Photodisc/Getty Images, p. 90; FotoRequest/Shutterstock, p. 92; John L. Absher/Shutterstock, p. 93; JumKit/Shutterstock, p. 94; Wataru Utada/Shutterstock, p. 97; kuvona/Shutterstock, p. 98; stonerobertc/iStock/Getty Images, p. 99; tome213/Shutterstock, p. 100; artisteer/iStock/Getty Images, p. 102; qushe/Shutterstock, p. 103; Laszlo66/Shutterstock, p. 104; Valerie Loiseleux/iStock/Getty Images, p. 105; Gemenacom/Shutterstock, p. 106; Usa-yon/Shutterstock, p. 107; Davdeka/Shutterstock, p. 108 (blue clouds). zorina_larisa/Shutterstock (design elements throughout). Cover: Kichigin/Shutterstock.com (bee); GCapture/Shutterstock.com (strawberries); Elovich/Shutterstock.com (blueberries); salajean/Shutterstock.com (sunflowers); languste/Shutterstock.com (chameleon); V J Matthew/Shutterstock.com (apples).

© 2020 Crayola, Easton, PA 18044-0431. Crayola Oval Logo, Crayola, Serpentine Design, Radical Red, Laser Lemon, Unmellow Yellow, Banana Mania, Asparagus, Granny Smith Apple, Screamin' Green, Wild Blue Yonder, Blue Bell, and Denim are registered trademarks of Crayola used under license.

Official Licensed Product
Lerner Publications Company
An imprint of Lerner Publishing Group, Inc.
241 First Avenue North
Minneapolis, MN 55401 USA

For reading levels and more information, look up this title at www.lernerbooks.com.

Main body text set in Mikado Medium.
Typeface provided by HVD Fonts.

Library of Congress Cataloging-in-Publication Data

The Cataloging-in-Publication Data for *Our Colorful World: A Crayola® Celebration of Color*
    is on file at the Library of Congress.

Manufactured in China
1-47445-48011-6/26/2019